I0530740

ROBERT TURNER

PULP FICTION

LEGACY EDITION

THE LOST WRITING MANUAL
OF 1948

SURRENDER
POINT
PRESS
LEXINGTON, KENTUCKY USA

Surrender Point Press
an imprint of dFRAE Media Co.

www.dfraemedia.com
North Hollywood, California USA

Copyright © 2025 by dFRAE Media Company

Provenance of Underlying Text and Illustrations

Book Design & Art Direction by David Franklin Sparks
Typeset in Spectral, a typeface designed by Production Type. Licensed
under the SIL Open Font License, Version 1.1.
Cover illustration is a modern artistic creation in the pulp-era style. The
illustrations featured within are authentic covers from the period.
ISBN 979-8-89965-659-0 (Paperback)
ISBN 979-8-89860-068-6 (E-book)

PUBLISHER'S NOTE

Some writers get spoken about like they handed down truth on stone tablets. Robert Turner is not one of those, and he'd have laughed at anyone who tried to put him there.

Turner (1915–1980) was a hustler in the honest sense of the word. He worked out the game early: you don't survive on art, you survive on output. Over thirty-two years he put something like ten million words on paper. Detective stories. Westerns. Romance. TV scripts. Whatever was buying that month, he was selling it, and the typewriter never seemed to cool off.

What he understood, and what a lot of writing

teachers still don't, is that the reader mostly wants to be entertained. To feel something. To get a few dozen pages away from their own life. All the theory in the world won't save a story that lies dead on the page, and Turner was not in the business of dead pages.

He learned the trade in the pulps. *Manhunt. Dime Detective. Thrilling Detective. Crack Detective.* The names alone sound like a cocktail list from a bar in Hell's Kitchen. He wasn't precious about any of it. He wrote stories with titles like "Abra Cadaver!" and "Hook, Line and Sucker!" and never pretended they were anything grander than what they were.

But here's what lifts him out of the crowd of working stiffs: he learned to edit, too. By thirty-three he'd already sold north of five hundred stories. He'd also worked as an editor and a literary agent, which gave him a view of the business most writers never get. When he took over *The Spider* in 1943, he did what he called "heavy rewriting" on other people's work, dragging their stiff, old-fashioned pulp style toward something with a pulse. He was teaching old dogs how to make a reader care.

His 1948 how-to, *Pulp Fiction: The First Manual of Modern Pulp Fiction*, is the book you're holding. For decades it was practically a rumor, surviving in a handful of crumbling copies. In the late 1990s a book scout named John Grow turned one up in a dusty used bookstore, and that fragile little manual is more or less why this reprint exists. What makes it worth reading now is how plainly Turner talks. No academic fog. Just his belief that the whole job is emotional engagement, that you write real people instead of stock cutouts, and that you write like you mean it rather than to a formula.

When the pulps started dying in the 1950s, Turner didn't write an elegy. He followed the money to television, part of that wave of hard-nosed pros shipped out to Hollywood to feed the script machine. *Alfred Hitchcock Presents. Johnny Midnight. Mike Hammer.* The medium changed; the hustle didn't.

People who knew him called him a "Dutch uncle," the kind who handed out advice with a dry wit and no pretension. He called himself a hack with zero shame, because to him "hack" was a job description, not a wound. He wasn't chasing awards. He was chasing the next check and was honest enough to say so. He trusted his gut over any rulebook, and he knew the value of underplaying a moment, of indirection, of making the reader lean in and do a little of the work.

The man also read constantly, taking other people's

stories apart to see what made them run. His advice to beginners was about as practical as advice gets: start small, five thousand words or less, and make every one of them earn its place.

His range was almost comic. When he wasn't writing detectives he was inventing characters for Quality Comics, ghost-writing Shaft novels, and turning out Mafia paperbacks under an invented Italian name. He could put on whatever skin the assignment called for.

In 1970 he published his autobiography under the title *Some of My Best Friends Are Writers But I Wouldn't Want My Daughter to Marry One*, which tells you everything about how he saw the trade.

He died in 1980, and for a while it looked like the world had filed him under forgotten. Pulp had gone out of fashion. But the real hustlers tend to get dug back up eventually.

This reprint keeps Turner's original text intact, plain-spoken voice and all. It's rooted in the specific machinery of 1940s magazine publishing, sure, but what he says about building characters, running a plot, and surviving as a working writer hasn't aged much at all.

Turner never wrote the Great American Novel. He was too busy writing a hundred pretty good ones that kept the lights on. He wasn't the most profound man ever to sit at a typewriter, and he'd have been the first to say so. He was just the one who kept turning pages and kept giving readers a reason to ask for the next one.

And now, here's *Pulp Fiction* by Robert Turner.

—David Sparks, Publisher

CONTENTS

To Peggy, whose loyalty and inspiration have made this man's writing career whatever it is and whatever it shall be.

ABOUT THE AUTHOR

R OBERT TURNER IS 33 years old and has been writing professionally for ten years. He has sold over 500 scripts of all types and lengths. It took him three years and over a hundred rejections before he sold his first story to a now defunct publication called *Tattle Tales* for the sum of $13.50, which at the time looked like a million. He has since then received as high as forty cents a word for a slick magazine short story.

He has also served as an editor at *Popular Publications, Inc.*, and *Ace Magazines, Inc.*, where he purchased hundreds of manuscripts for such magazines as *Detective Tales*, *Big Book Western*, *Western Aces*, and *Ten-Story Detective*; and as a literary agent.

When not chained to a typewriter and under surveillance by his wife and two daughters, Turner, an avid fishing fan, takes off for the lake near his New Jersey home. While thinking up plots for his stories, he lies prone upon the studio couch in his den, with eyes closed and mouth open. Some observers have confused this plotting technique with the gentle art of sleeping. Which is ridiculous, Turner says, yawning and waking up.

INTRODUCTION

T HIS IS NOT A textbook on how to write. I am not
a teacher. For that very reason, perhaps there
will be some things I can tell you that an instructor
on the subject of writing cannot. I would like this
little book to be a sort of personal talk from me on
the specialized subject of pulp fiction writing. It will
attempt to advise you on certain points, to simplify
and strip some of the obscurity and confusion away
from certain so-called technical aspects of writing a
fiction story.

Although I will deal here mostly with pulp fiction,
a lot of the things I say will apply to all fields of sto-

ry-telling: so, if writers other than pulpsters read this and get something out of it, that is all to the good. But it is intended, primarily, to help those writers trying to break into the pulp field, with the intention of making pulp fiction writing their career or a stepping stone to smooth paper and novel sales. At the same time, I have hopes that it will also come to the attention of the many writers who sell once in a while, whose sales average is not too high—and perhaps give them a hand toward getting less rejects and more checks.

If this book is read by any professionals, I hope they will be kind and not make me blush too damned hard next time I see them. I will go so far as to say that I hope perhaps even they will get something out of this work—even if it is only something that they already know but have long since forgotten and about which they need to be reminded. I have hopes for this because I know that I would be bound to get something out of a book on writing, turned out by some of them. None of us knows it all.

There will be some guys, of course, who will say that I am a large sized damned fool to give away any of the tricks of our trade. They will say the profession is already crowded enough, that every week there are newcomers breaking into the books, charged up as all hell and setting the pulp world on fire with their stuff, without adding to our discomfort.

To that I answer: Those newcomers would do it anyway, whether you or I do anything to help them or not. They are just plain good. I also firmly believe that there aren't any of us who, when we were breaking in, weren't helped in some way by some guy or gal already arrived, either in the form of a book or article on how to write, or by personal assistance. I know I was. There were many, many professionals who were very kind and who helped a lot toward getting me started. I feel that it will not do any harm to make repayment in kind, as best I can.

In this manual, I have tried to stay away from the tested, tried and true methods of textbook instruction on how to write. You will probably find some disorder, but I don't think that is important. There have been many books written which deal with the subject of writing and start off by telling you that a story must have three parts: a beginning, a middle and an ending. I have assumed that you already know or suspect such things.

What I have mainly tried to do here is to answer questions, which you, as a presently or potentially serious commercial fiction writer, with no delusions about writing long-haired art, might like to ask of an established writer in your field, if you had the chance. You would be asking these questions, I assume, because they have not been answered elsewhere.

What this book lacks in size, I hope that it makes up by being fairly meaty in contents. I could easily have made it longer, I assure you. I could have padded this book to full length and had it put between hard covers and a publisher could have soaked you three bucks for it. But there would have been no more actual benefit in it for you. By doing it this way, I have tried to take up less of your time and mine, and have thus cost you less money, and will, perhaps, sell a great many more copies. In the long run, the whole thing should balance out and everybody will be happy.

—Robert Turner

I

F IRST OF ALL, IN the past ten years, the word "pulp" as applied to magazines, has become a misnomer. To the average person, and surprisingly enough, to many writers, all pulp magazines are supposed to contain nothing but sensational blood and thunder trash. They think that pulp writers are hacks and that no "good" or really competent literary craftsman would allow his work to appear in such a medium. The term, "the pulps," has become synonymous with cheap and flashy writing.

At one time, many years ago, in the diaper days of the pulp publishing business, this reaction had some basis in fact. But not today.

The modern pulp magazine is so far removed from its earlier prototype, that it should no longer be forced to bear the same label. No more than modern motion pictures should still be referred to as "flickers" or "talkies". But the nick-name will probably persist, purely because this type of magazine is still printed on a coarse grade of paper manufactured from wood pulp.

This, by the way, is not an effort to defend the pulps; they need no defense. They have become an American institution, beloved by millions of readers. But among the readers of this book, there will be some who do not recognize this fact. They will be laboring under the false premise that the pulps are the burlesque circuit of the writing business. They have been afraid to write pulp for fear of tarnishing their possible future reputation. Others, potentially successful pulp fictioneers if they had not been suffering under this delusion, have tried but failed to crack the field for that very reason. They have been writing down, forcing themselves to write bad stories because they thought that was what pulp editors wanted. Nothing could be farther from the truth. Such writers have been cheating themselves out of a possibly lucrative and respectable career.

If they will go out and buy and read some of the top paying, better class, modern pulps, they will be in for a surprise. They will learn that the word pulp does not go hand in hand with trashy writing. They will learn that they can write as fine and smooth prose as they desire, provided they weave it carefully around a solidly constructed plot—and pulp editors will start buying from them so fast it will make their heads spin. By "solidly constructed plot," I do not necessarily mean fanciful, over-sensational, wild and woolly, unbelievable story machinations. The plot of a pulp yarn can be realistic and sometimes slight, so long as it has the compensations of strong characterization, atmosphere and dramatic impact.

The main difference between the pulps and other fields of writing such as the slicks and even "literary" novels—is not in the writing or handling, but only in that one word, plot. The pulp story must have some semblance of a plot. The other fields of writing do not always insist on this. You can sometimes sell a slick magazine story that is purely a sketch, plotless. You can even sell a book publisher a plotless jumble of words, providing it is entertaining in some way.

But in absolutely no field of writing does the ability

to plot injure a writer's reputation nor his chances to go to the very top. In fact, it will help him no end. Many of our big-name slick writers, our currently best-selling novelists and the old time authors of some of our very greatest literary classics, are or were top-grade plotsmiths. Their ability to write a plotted story and wrap it well in good smooth prose has been their forte. Take Clarence Budington Kelland, Ben Ames Williams and Charles Dickens, as examples.

If you aspire to writing for the slicks or for the novel field, rest assured that putting in an apprenticeship in the pulps will do you much more good than harm, in every way that really counts. It will teach you how to plot; it will help you to polish up your prose until it is finally good enough for both pulp and slick. At which point you will promptly switch over to selling your best stories to the slicks instead of the pulps for the simple reason that they will pay you more per story, not because your writing has become too good for the pulps.

Just in case I gave you the wrong impression by saying that you will have to plot to sell pulps and that you can sometimes sell a slick magazine story or produce a best selling novel without plotting, let me steer you back onto the right road. You can sell a slick magazine story—and if you're really lucky, perhaps even a novel—that is almost entirely without a plot. But don't say: "Then why the hell should I bother with plotting and the pulps, when I can sit down and knock out a beautiful little character sketch for Collier's or Good Housekeeping?"

Unless you are a pure genius, you will find it almost impossible to do a "plotless" story that is well written enough and entertaining enough to sell to the big time, without first putting in years of effort and practice. That is doing it the hard way. It is much simpler to learn something about plotting and about writing first and sell enough pulp and slick material to establish your name and to develop your skill to the point where you can turn out and sell one of those deceptively simple-appearing character sketches that you sometimes see in the big name magazines. For every "plotless" story they buy, they purchase at least a thousand plotted stories.

Of course if you are a genius, either pure or otherwise, that is another matter. I'm afraid reading this book will not do you much good and if you will write me, and tell me that you are a genius, I, personally, will refund your purchase price.

Now, I hope we have established the fact that if you

are going to write for the pulp magazines, you do not have to, and cannot, look down your nose at them, nor write down for them. Instead, you will write the best piece of prose fiction of which you are capable, and make sure it contains a carefully worked out and believable plot.

This matter of attitude is of utmost importance. I know from experience as an agent and as a pulp magazine editor that many potentially good writers fail to crack the pulp market—or any market—because of the wrong attitude. I know of writers, obviously capable of doing really fine stories, who not let themselves do so because they falsely believed that the pulps wanted crude, hyped-up, ridiculously plotted blood-and-thunder tales. Once they were straightened out on this score, they became convinced that the market would take the best things they could write: they began selling almost immediately.

Let that sink in. The first step toward writing successful pulp fiction is a proper attitude and respect for the medium.

The second important step is to read and study the work of writers who appear regularly in the top grade, better paying pulps. Read current pulp magazines, not a copy of Dragnet, from the year 1927, which you happen to find buried in the attic. In this reading and studying phase of your career, you will find out for yourself what fine writing and excellent and entertaining stories appear in modern pulp magazines.

A NOVEL OF THE FUTURE COMPLETE IN THIS ISSUE!

STARTLING STORIES

15¢

FALL ISSUE

A THRILLING PUBLICATION

Aftermath
An Amazing Complete Novel
By JOHN RUSSELL FEARN

SUPERMAN OF DR. JUKES
A Hall of Fame Classic
By FRANCIS FLAGG

BUY WAR BONDS AND STAMPS FOR VICTORY!

STARTLING STORIES, 1945

2

THERE ARE, AS YOU know, subdivisions of the pulp magazine field. They are, mainly: the detective group, the westerns, the love group and the sports group. In addition, there are a few science-fiction magazines and books featuring air-war stories; several "adventure" magazines (which use all kinds of male-interest stories—detective, western, sports, historical and sometimes a fantasy piece, all together in the same magazine), and a few magazines using a combination of western-and-love type of stories, known as the western romance group.

Although these specialized pulps, such as Adventure, Astounding Science-Fiction, Short Stories, Weird Tales, Rangeland Romances, etc., are old established markets, enjoying considerable prestige and featuring the work of many very well known writers, your target is very, very small if you aim at them. Unless you hit the bull's eye in the first couple of shots, you are liable to wind up with a dud reject on your hands. The field is too narrow for the beginning writer. You might as well put the odds on your side.

For instance, you write an historical-costume piece of fiction, or an air-war yarn, or a fantasy piece, or a western love story, and after a couple of submissions and several rejects, you are through. But take a whack at the whopping big detective, western, sports or love pulp fields and the law of averages moves over onto your side. If you miss out with the first several submissions at the top of the field, you can still run on through at least a dozen or more other publications, all of which use stories of a similar type.

It's okay to take an experimental flier, once in a while, into one of these more or less specialized fields of pulp, but your best bet for concentrated effort will be to batter steadily at the doors of the four major pulp divisions. With proper study and application, you should eventually hit one group, or several, or even all of these major pulp groups, fairly regularly.

The first and foremost of all these pulp groups is, in my estimation, the detective field. I'm going out on a limb with this statement and leaving myself wide open to argument. I suppose every writer specializing in one of the other fields will come running at me, wild-eyed and with axe in hand.

I'll try to support that statement. In the first place, detective story readers are, I believe, a little more discriminating than any other types They demand more in the way of characterization and emotional impact in their reading matter. These are two of the most difficult products for a writer to deliver consistently.

The detective story reader is not particularly fascinated by any one particular type of action or background or costume, or by story props in themselves, such as cowboy suits and horses and mass gunfights. He cannot be dazzled into overlooking plot flaws or weaknesses in characterization or sameness of theme by detailed, play-by-play description of a sports contest; or by hard-riding and gun-fighting; or by the romantic, emotional fencing of a beautiful female and a handsome male.

Not that I have anything against the western, sports or love pulp fields. All of them have been very kind to me. I know that western story writers will hurl Ernest Haycox and Zane Gray and Luke Short at me. The sports and love story writers will proudly display one of their alumni who has gone on to higher paying fields. That is fine. I know that good writing is not limited to any one field. But I do feel and believe that you will find more good writing and a greater number of talented writers in the crime-detective group of pulps than in any other.

Perhaps I feel so strongly about this subject, and have such great respect for the detective type of story, in any of its many forms, because it was the field in which I first tried my own wings. For much too long I batted my head against the doors of the detective pulp magazines. I became bowed and bloody, doing so. You can't help but feel very respectful for a guy who gives you a terrific fight before you lick him. And I firmly believe that if I had tried to break into one of the other fields first, I would have made my first sale a hell of a lot sooner.

Nevertheless, I'm going to suggest that if you have yet to make your first sale and if you like crime or detective stories—and if you have guts—that you do exactly the same thing. Take a big, healthy swing at the detective fiction pulps, right off the bat. If you make it, fine. If you learn to write well enough to crack that most difficult of all pulp fields, first off, you will never have too much trouble breaking into any of the others.

If, after a good struggle, it is obvious that you cannot make this group, then go after one of the other groups. You will find them one hundred percent easier to break into, by comparison. It is something like hitting yourself over the head with a hammer because it feels so good when you stop.

I know many successful crime-fiction writers who have later broken into other fields with comparative ease and great success. I know of others who have switched almost entirely to westerns or sports or both, because they have found them so much easier to write—and to sell. But I know of comparatively few western or sports pulpateers who have switched to the detective group with any great measure of success.

The story ingredients of all groups, by the way, are practically the same—but they have to be mixed—and used—with much greater skill in the detective story.

Another good reason for learning to master the crime story first (the chances are that is the only way in which you'll master it) is that more big names in the slick, novel, radio and motion picture fields have come out of the detective group than any other type of pulps. Writing crime fiction is the best training in the world toward breaking into those greener pastures.

And speaking of those greener pastures, just in case you might be still laboring under the delusion that there's no future in writing pulp fiction, that you're going to "ruin" your writing style, or hurt your name, or that your friends and relatives are going to be ashamed of you, or some other such silly nonsense—right now might be a good time to really set you straight.

Did you ever hear of Major George Fielding Eliot, the commentator and military news analyst? Thomas W. Duncan, author of the best seller, "Gus The Great?" Or Steve Fisher? (I've just read in a Hollywood column that he is getting $75,000 for doing his next screen play.) Or George Bruce, screen playwright and producer? Dashiell Hammett, Raymond Chandler, Cornell Woolrich (William Irish)? Or the well known slick magazine writers, Frederick Nebel, William E. Barrett, William Fay, Roderick Lull, Willard H. Temple, Thomas Walsh, Wyatt Blassingame, Kenneth Perkins, Richard Sale, P G. Wodehouse, Agatha Christie, Rudyard Kipling, Sinclair Lewis? Well, all of those names—and I could go on down the page with many, many more—at one time or another wrote pulp fiction. I believe most of them would readily admit it. Many of them would be proud to do so.

It keeps right on happening, too. Many of our leading pulpsters are even now reaching the point where their finished fiction products are so good that they'll sell to either slick or pulp. For instance, I pick up a couple of the big circulation, smooth paper magazines on my desk right now, scan the contents page, and find Henry Norton in one and William Holder in another. Norton has written hundreds of very fine pulp crime pieces. Holder has turned out reams of sports pulp fiction under several pseudonyms. You will be hearing a lot from these boys in the future, and many others who will from time to time pop right out of the pulp pages.

Which brings us back to you. You can do the same thing, and make a damned fine living—or spare time money—while you're doing it, if you go at it the right way. If you have no ambitions toward the smooth paper or novel or motion picture fields, you can stay right in the pulps for the rest of your life and do very nicely for yourself. I know pulpsteers who have been in the business ten, fifteen and twenty years—who are making from $5,000 to $15,000 a year—who have no desire to leave the field. Who can blame them?

I say that you can in all likelihood make good in the pulps because I am assuming that you are of average intelligence and can read and write good English and can pound a typewriter with a fair degree of skill. These things, plus the right attitude, plus a willingness to study and learn, are the only basic requirements any man or woman needs to be able to write and sell a piece of pulp fiction. All other abilities necessary can be acquired. The degree of success in the field will, of course, depend on the individual and how badly he wants to succeed.

What I am getting at is that you do not have to be any special type or kind of a guy or gal. You do not have to be inspired. You do not have to be an introvert or an extrovert or even intellectual. You do not have to be either tall or short, fat or lean. You do not have to be a Harvard graduate. You do not have to be a genius. You do not have to be a world traveler.

Fiction writers fit into all types and categories, just as do folks in other trades or professions. Some of them are heels. Some are the salt of the earth. Some are big-mouthed bores. Others are meek little Caspar Milquetoasts. Some are handsome; some ugly as sin.

The only thing that counts in the fiction writing racket, brethren and sistern, is what you do with words when you sit down in front of a typing machine. Words are the tools of your trade and you must know how to use them. That is the one MUST. I don't mean that you have to possess the vocabulary of a lexicographer. Plain, simple, ordinary, everyday words are enough. If you have read a lot from the time you were a kid—and if you haven't, chances are that you wouldn't be interesting in being a writer, anyhow—your vocabulary will see you through. So if you only finished the sixth or eighth grade, forget about it. Plenty of other writers are in the same boat. Sometimes I believe that not being exposed to too much formal education is an advantage.

MAMMOTH MYSTERY, 1947

3

I SUPPOSE BY THIS time you are wondering when in hell I am going to get to the subject of technique. How do I write pulp fiction, you say? That's a good question and I am in the process of trying to answer it for you. I have been trying from page one of this book. But I have been approaching it in a slightly different way. You might say that I'm sneaking up on you with it.

I am not fond of the word technique. There have been many books, many articles—millions of words—written on the subject of technique. Too many of them by folks not really qualified. I know.

Very early in what I fondly call my career, I swallowed and gagged and got literary indigestion on practically all of these books. You, too, have probably read more of them than you should, already. Your head must be swimming with catch phrases such as "theme," "conflict," "introspection," "stream-of consciousness," "viewpoints," "structure," "denouement," "harmony of viewpoint," ad nauseam. I shall probably have to resort to a few of those terms myself before I am through, but I hope to do it painlessly. I do not want to confuse you any more than you are, already.

So I say, right here and now, phooey to technique, as such. Too much importance has been attached to the bare mechanics of story structure and not enough to injecting life and blood into a yarn and making it pure and simple entertainment.

If you have not already fueled up your brain on the subject of technique in writing, do not look for it here. I can recommend a very good book, The Dynamics Of Drama by George Armin Shaftel. This is not a plug for a friend. I do not even know the gentleman. But I do know that he qualifies to write a book on fiction technique, because he has, himself, written and sold many pulp and slick magazine stories.

The trouble with most of the rules of writing technique is that these very rules can be—and sometimes should be—broken, in order to make a story salable. To be salable, a story must first be readable. To be readable, it must be entertaining. It's really quite simple.

But how in hell can your story be entertaining, if every moment that you spent creating it, you were constantly sweating and straining to make it technically perfect inasmuch as "the man in the book" said it should be? Writing a story is not like putting together a kid's bicycle or a patented can opener. There are no sets of instructions. Thank God. If there were, everybody would be writing successfully and there wouldn't be a living in it for any of us.

What I am trying to give you here are points that I never found in any of the books on technique. Some of the things might take you three or four years to find out via the trial and error method, by butting your head against a wall of rejection slips. Things you won't learn from shuffling through a deck of cards with purported segments of plots printed on the back of them, or through literary graphs and charts or mechanical gadgets. Folks, writing a story is not as simple as spinning a cardboard wheel.

Did you ever come up against a book of writing

technique that came right out and said: "Look, Joe, for Hell's sake, forget all this guff about plot structure and be downright, just plain, ordinary entertaining."? Well, that's the main rule of fiction writing, for my money. That is the idea.

Figure it this way: you want some jaded editor to be intrigued into reading your story all the way through. If that happens, he in turn figures that the magazine's readers will also be intrigued. That is the way he measures your story—or should—if he is a good or successful editor.

His job is to judge whether or not your typewritten manuscript, when fancied up with a provocative title, blurb and illustration, will keep some poor guy on a train entertained between visits to the club car bar. Or some gal awake while she sits up and waits for her husband to come home from his night out with "the boys." Or to help some bank president escape from his own conscience by temporarily associating himself with some poor devil in a hell of a fiction mess.

This editor judges whether or not your story will accomplish this bit of business by its overall effect on him. He doesn't—or shouldn't—judge it by checking to see if you've followed all the rules in fiction writing, as set down by Joe Blow in his textbook, "How To

Write." Especially since he damned well knows Joe Blow, himself, couldn't make a living writing salable fiction, if he had it to do.

It is because all pulp writing aspirants fill their manuscripts with as many of these Joe Blow textbook rules as they can cram onto twenty pieces of bond paper that the slush pile in every editorial office is a thing of horror to the poor guy who has to wade through it.

Stop trying to impress an editor with all the rules of writing technique that you have been forced to swallow. Stop trying to pack into every 5,000 words of script all the things you think the editor wants to find there. You will then be about twenty laps ahead of the average tyro. Try to entertain the guy, not just show off your technical know-how.

This may sound like double-talk, I know. But it isn't. Sure, sure, you say, okay, I'll write an entertaining story and to hell with all the rules and regulations. Okay, we're right back at the beginning again. How, friend Turner, HOW?

Now that you've got me pinned down, I'll try to deliver the goods. I'm going to seem to pile on the double talk by giving you some other rules to follow. But hold on. These are not rules of writing technique, as such. They are rules and laws of human nature and comparatively simple. Follow them and your chances of writing a piece of entertainment—which is all that a story is—will be increased a thousandfold.

I hope you know what emotions are, because they play a prominent part in this not so gentle art of fiction writing. You, as a writer, are going to play on emotions, with words, as a pianist tickles the ivory keys with his fingers. At least, you are if you intend to succeed as a fiction writer.

We all have emotions. Prod any reader's emotional reflexes and, Mr. and Mrs. Writer, you are going to entertain him. I am not a psychologist, so perhaps my definitions of these terms will not be technically correct. But they will serve the purpose to show you what I am getting at, I think.

To me, the condition of being entertained is a comparative state. It is being aware, the opposite of being bored. If you needle a reader's emotions, he cannot be bored. There are many ways to do this. The more of them that you learn, the more powerful and successful a writer you will become. That is why, forever after you have sold your first story, you will constantly study people and other writer's work, to learn more and more of the tricks of getting at people's emotions.

Examples are sometimes good for clarification. Okay. Let's say that you love dogs. You are walking along the street and you see some guy kicking the hell out of some skinny, half starved little pooch. Or some sadistic guttersnipe is tying tin cans onto a puppy's tail. What do you feel? It can be anger, or sympathy, or both. Those are emotions.

All right, there are two nice little emotions all lined up and dusted off for you. Use them in a story. Substitute the villain or one of his henchmen for the guy doing the kicking in the example used. Substitute your hero—or heroine—for the pooch. I've started many a story that's sold, with the hero getting hell beat out of him—or just coming out of unconsciousness and pulling himself to his feet, after taking a shellacking. The reader feels sorry for the character, he feels sympathy toward him. You have aroused an emotion; therefore, you are entertaining the reader.

To do this properly, of course, you have to build a scene that comes alive in the reader's mind. That hinges on the subject of realism and we will deal with that in due time. In the street scene example, something is really happening and you damned well know that, because you can hear the dog squealing or whining and you can hear the guy cussing and the sound of his boot connecting with the animal's ribs. In the story scene, you've got to kid the reader into thinking it is actually happening. We will cover that, later.

Now, for Job's sake, please don't start every story from here on in, with some poor guy getting the be-jabbers beat out of him. That is only one way to arouse one emotion in a reader. There are hundreds—perhaps thousands—of other ways.

Here we go again: another example, another emotion. In fact a couple of them. We'll combine a couple of emotions in one example and hope you don't get confused. There is already enough confusion in this business of learning how to write, without my adding to it.

Let's say you are walking along a busy thoroughfare and a couple of kids are playing ball on the sidewalk. Suddenly the ball goes out into the street. One of the kids, unthinking, dashes out from between parked cars, after the ball. You see this. You see him run blindly out into the middle of traffic after that ball. You see one speeding car swerve and narrowly miss him. You hear the screeching of brakes. You see another car bearing down upon the boy. He suddenly becomes aware of his predicament, tries to dodge the speeding cars. Watching this, what do you feel? Fear and anxiety for the boy's safety. There are a couple of emotions. They are sometimes coupled under the word "suspense," which is a favorite term in a lot of books on how to write. If you happen to know this boy, your fear and anxiety for his safety is increased. If he is a nephew, say, your emotions become even stronger. If he is your own son...!

But here we are getting mixed up in the subject of characterization which must also come later. Characterization is merely making your reader more aware of what happens to your characters, because you make him feel that he knows them, recognizes them and thereby you increase his emotional reactions to what happens to the characters. How to perform that little trick comes later in the act.

Now, let's get back to our street scene. The boy caught in the middle of speeding traffic suddenly jumps out of the way of one car—and right smack into the path of another. He is hit, knocked down. The fear and anxiety emotions now leave you, or they are modified to some extent by how badly is the boy hurt?

Suddenly, from a nearby house, a woman rushes out screaming. Traffic is now stopped. A crowd has gathered around the prone figure of the boy who has been hit. The woman pushes through the crowd, sobbing, hysterical. It is obvious that she is the boy's mother. She kneels beside him. You feel another emotion, pity.

I don't believe I have to delve much farther into this subject. We assumed, to begin with, that you have average intelligence. What I'm getting at, must have become obvious by this time. You must know what I mean by the word, emotions. Now all you have to do, with your little typewriter, is to play upon a certain number of these emotions in a story. Play on them hard. Make your reader laugh, make him cry, make him sigh and you can forget about plot complications and mechanical rules, as set forth in text books on how to write. While you are playing hard on one of your reader's emotions, you are keeping him from being bored. You are entertaining him.

Only watch your timing. Emotions harden. If you stay too long, fooling around with one particular emotion, or keep working on the same one in the same way, too many times, it will lose its effect. If you saw a child knocked down by a car every day for a long period, if this were a usual, ordinary occurrence, your emotions would become numbed; they would harden.

Vary the emotion-rousing tunes you play on your

typewriter. There are so many of them. Anger, fear, frustration, pity, indignation, anxiety, terror, are only a few. There are many shades to each one. I cannot take these tools and use them for you. I can only try to show them to you. You will have to take them up and learn to use them, with ever increasing skill, yourself. You will have to put these emotional stimulants, in one way or another, into your stories. Do that and you will have the editors—and the readers—by the short hairs.

From here on in, when you read a story in a magazine, do not read for your own entertainment, alone. Try to analyze just which way your own emotions were played upon by the author, and which ones he needled. Make a study of this business of emotions. Don't fight them in yourself. Encourage them. React to them. In that way you will learn much about them and how to use them to evoke the same reactions in other people.

I hope by this time that you have about accepted the fact that to entertain a reader—in other words to write a good story—is to play upon emotions, through the things that you make happen to your story characters. Now, I'd like to get on to the characters themselves and the bugaboo subject of characterization. It is really not so bad, when you chew right into it and ignore the mildewed crust of stuffy and confusing wordage that has been written on the subject.

I don't, by the way, have any ridiculous notion that I am expounding any new and original theory of fiction writing. It's the same old theory that I'm preaching, that has been used by successful fictioneers for generations, from the first wandering street story teller up to and including the current, smoothly polished book club novelist.

This is all known very well by every fiction writer who ever received a publisher's check. Or at least he is aware of it, either consciously or subconsciously. I'm sure the good word has been passed on here and there or has been rooted out by newcomers in the business in some way or another.

All I'm endeavoring to do, is clear away some of the cobwebs from these true basic principles of story writing; some of the protective coloration that has grown around it; some of the camouflage that has been draped over it, somewhere along the line.

THRILLING DETECTIVE, 1948

FIGHT STORIES, 1949

4

STORY CHARACTERS ARE PEOPLE. That may sound a bit silly on the surface and I'll have to elaborate on the subject, I know. What I mean to say is, keep them human! Your editor and your reader wants to recognize them, to identify himself or herself with these characters. He cannot do this if they react in completely unbelievable ways. Your story characters, also, must have emotions, the same as your reader. Your characters have to react emotionally to given situations in a realistic manner or they do not come alive to the reader.

Before we go any farther on this subject I'd like to

touch lightly upon some of the tricks and methods that I have seen and read and heard advocated, from time to time, regarding characterization. There are many. Most of them, I, personally, have found useless.

I have read that you should make a dossier of the characters in your story. You should know them, it says. You should be able—and some instructors go so far as to tell you actually to do it—to write a life history of each important character in your story. That's an intriguing idea, if you care for that sort of thing. If you have the time.

(Personally, if I had to do that every time I write a story, I would go back to punching somebody's time clock, but fast, and to hell with this business. Perhaps that system does work for some people. If it does—if it works for you—fine. Stick to it. I'm going to try to show you a simpler method of creating believable characters, but that doesn't mean you have to use it.)

Then there is the favorite advice of "tagging" or "labeling" your characters. Also nice going—and very fine—if you can get away with it. The first time I heard of this idea, many years ago, I was fascinated by it. The next story I wrote had every character in it either flipping a coin, munching on sunflower seeds, pulling at his earlobe, wearing squeaky shoes, twirling a watchchain, biting his fingernails and so on. You know what happened to that story, so full of "tags" and "labels" it looked like a trunk whose owner had just come back from a round-the-world cruise. My only consolation is that as an editor and later, an agent, I learned that I wasn't the only beginning writer who had done something like that.

In the next story, I calmed down a bit and only "tagged" a couple of lead characters. But I gave them such outlandish labels that they became completely unbelievable to the reader. He could no longer identify himself with some jerk hero who went around continually straightening pictures on everybody's walls, or something like that. There was no point in it. He simply irritated the reader. Of course, if this habit of straightening pictures led the hero eventually to find a secret safe hidden behind one of them, or something like that but that is another matter again.

What I am getting at, is, that a rule such as "tag your character and then parade that tag for all it is worth," tossed, unqualified, at a beginning writer, is sometimes a little rough on the guy. He is liable to find himself hanging onto the tail of a leaping steer that will throw him all over hell-and-gone before he lets go.

Sure, you can tag some characters and make it effective. But you've got to be careful how you do it. It is rather, it seems to me, an advanced trick that needs to be handled expertly, a sharp and dangerous tool in the hands of somebody who is not familiar with its usage. So, if you want to fool around with that little stunt, or any of the others you've read or heard about, go ahead. They might work for you. They didn't for me, nor for a lot of other writers I know.

My personal advice is again to toss the rule book out the window. Instead of following the laws of technique, get down to the fundamentals of human nature. Humanize your characters. Make them in most ways just like you and me—and the editor—and the reader. I once dealt on this subject, in considerable detail in an article in Writer's Digest, called "Real People In Crime."

Rogers Terrill, who was at that time managing editor of a string of Popular Publications' most successful pulps, paid me one of the greatest compliments I've ever had. He said that article was one of the best pieces on the subject of writing crime fiction that he'd ever seen. He said that it summed up, better than he could say it, himself, the policy on the kind of fiction he liked to run in Detective Tales—or some such thing.

I believe him because Rog isn't the kind of guy to kid you by tossing bouquets in your face and because at that time I was hitting Detective Tales, one of his leading magazines, month after month, consistently. I believed that I hit the nail on the head in that article on characterization in pulp stories because Rog is one of the greatest magazine editors in the publishing business.

I do not say that, by the way, because Terrill buys stories from me. He is now editor of the slick Argosy and I haven't yet hit that magazine.

Anyhow, to get back to the point, that Digest article dealt simply with the idea of making characters in a crime story "real people," not supermen or women. Your editor and your reader are not supermen and know of no such animal, so that they cannot identify themselves with any such creature. Nor were characters to be made simply wooden puppets, or gray, colorless blobs, moving through a set of situations.

I do not have that article at hand or I would quote directly from it. Somebody swiped it or it got thrown away by mistake, or something. But the general idea was this: Take somebody you know, think of your hero, say, as the guy next door, whom you've come to know pretty well. Give him some little human failings or weaknesses. Some of your own, perhaps, or your cousin, Louie's.

Maybe this guy likes the horses or the dice or a poker deck not wisely, but too well. Maybe he's unreasonably jealous of his young, pretty and rather dizzy wife. Any one of a million things like that. In other words, don't think of him as a, quote, story character, unquote, but as a living, breathing, human person, somebody you know!

Then expose him to an unusual and dramatic situation and let him carry the ball, from there on, with only a little casual guidance from you, as the author. Let him react to this dramatic situation as you would, yourself, or somebody that you know. Get inside your story characters while you are writing about them. Be them. Emotionalize with them and through them and you will convey the reality of that character, and his realistic reactions to the situation, to the reader. Then you will be entertaining the reader.

For instance, let's take this guy we've already started on. Because of his gambling debts, he's gotten into hot water with a loan shark, a "shylock." He's got a sum of money due on a certain date, or else. He knows the methods of this "shylock," what happens to welchers. Some night he'll be pulled into an alley and have the bejabbers knocked out of him. He's scared stiff. Wouldn't you be? And isn't such a situation humanly possible? It is, to use another favorite term of the textbook boys, "plausible." All that means is that your hero is in a situation that is not wildly imaginative, but something that could happen in real life. It springs from the character and one of his human weaknesses. It is not a wild and woolly, phony situation that you have cooked up, hoping to startle an editor out of his wits, to dazzle him. Believe me, he doesn't want to be startled or dazzled. He just wants to be moved, emotionally, so that he can be reasonably assured that his magazine's readers will react in the same way.

Now, let's move on to the "shylock." We'll make him a guy who goes for a pretty face and a well carved ankle. Isn't that believable? Doesn't that make him "real people"? Are you kidding?...All right. We have already established the fact that our poor hero's wife is young, pretty and dizzy. Isn't that in line with some gal you really know?

There's only one thing can happen, now. The "shylock" goes to the hero's house to try and collect his debt. He meets the pretty, dizzy young wife. He goes for the gal. He's in a good spot to put the pressure on her. He tries but the wife fights him off. Later, the husband hears about it. He's already established as an overly jealous guy. One emotion overcomes the other. The jealousy licks the fear. (You see, emotions, emotions all over the place!) He goes to the "shylock's" flat to tell him to leave his wife alone. If necessary, he's worked up enough even to take a whack at the stinker. What happens? He gets there and finds the guy dead. Somebody's killed him.

What's that? You can't plot? Brother, you don't have to plot. Start your plotting off by thinking in terms of your characters, keep them real, involve them in one real life situation and they'll take off and do your plotting for you. You can go on from the predicament in which we left that Joe, in any one of a dozen different ways, simply by getting inside of him and reacting emotionally with him. We act, most of us, through our emotions. That is, the act follows the emotion: You get sore at some guy and then you punch him. Make your characters real, human beings, with emotions and they'll lead you right into a story.

Take the same setup I used as an example—not a particularly good one, I agree, but adequate even though cooked up on the spur of the moment—and apply it to any one of the four major pulp groups and you will come up with a salable yarn. Which bears out the point I made earlier. The same basic ingredients go into all kinds of stories, detective, western, sport or love. They can come up smooth enough for slick, if you are skillful in your handling. That's a little detail we will touch upon, farther on in this manual; also—the pulp story that becomes good enough for both pulp and slick.

Just to hammer it in a little, to show you that story characters are all basically the same, and can be pushed into any one of the four major pulp types, let's examine, briefly, the sample characters and situations we used in that little crime story specimen. Shift the scene to the western cattle country, make the hero a rancher and the "shylock" a banker or "land-hog" and you can go into practically the same story.

Make your hero a ball player, with the same human weaknesses, and the "shylock" a bribe-offering gambler whom the hero visits to warn him away from the heroine, and you're off on a sports yarn. Tell the thing from the girl's viewpoint, keep her single, making the hero her boyfriend instead of her husband, make the "shylock" a wealthy and attractive young debutante, chuck out the crime and violence angles, and you can

ROBERT TURNER

be off on a love pulp yarn.

So much for characterization. No tricks, no gadgets, no wearying windup before the pitch, in the form of long drawn out dossiers on your characters. Just take your knowledge of human beings, fold in a few emotions, keep the whole thing real, believable. You don't need a lot of fancy pyrotechnics to attract the editor's attention to your characters. They don't have to jump and stomp around, or blow bubble gum. Just make a character some poor slob, with troubles and emotions, even as you and I.

One last thing on the subject. Description. That is, physical description. Stay away from stock types. All heroes aren't tall, dark and handsome, with Apollo-like builds, in real life. Don't make him a jerk, or repulsive. In your mind, get a picture of somebody you know fairly well, transfer that picture to your story. Don't go into minute detail with your descriptions. Highlight them.

You've seen drawings where a lot of parts are left out, but the features that are sketched in are done so deftly that your imagination fills in the rest and your mind gets a clear picture. For an exaggerated example, if someone drew an egg-shaped face, stuck a lock of hair down over one eye and a dab of black mustache, wouldn't you recognize it? No eyes, no nose, nothing but that hank of hair down over the forehead and a dab of mustache and you've got Hitler. That's what I mean, only not so obviously tagged. Just sketch in some high points of description on your characters, so that they form a picture for the reader, or enable him to form one, or associate it with someone he knows. Let him form his own picture of the hero—with your help. Don't try to paint the whole thing for him.

But do this character sketching with words, cleverly. Don't settle with calling the hero "a tall, good looking guy." Make it something like this. "He was big but a little gaunt looking, so that his clothes never seemed to fit him quite right. His lean, pleasantly homely face now held a drawn and harried look, etc." That's quick and rough, but I'm trying to give you the general idea.

Slip this description of a character to the reader, when the character first comes onto the scene. Don't wait until he's half way through the story—or even through several paragraphs. Throughout the story, dab in quick touches of that description, now and then. When this guy reacts with an emotion—and if he doesn't after the way I've harped on the subject, I give you up—as against some situation, flick in a lick of that description.

Another example:

> He looked down at Bruno, lying there,
> still and twisted and dead, upon the
> floor. For a moment the long, bony fea-
> tures of his face seemed to fall apart
> with shock. Then they tightened into
> an expression of horror. One corner of
> his wide mouth began to twitch. His big
> fists clenched and unclenched against
> his long, thin legs....

The description's there, and the character keeps
emoting. Your story characters are actors, always on
the stage. They just don't come out there and stand
and do nothing. Make them have emotions and react
to them. Then they will come alive. You will be writing a story, entertainment, not an exercise in fiction
writing technique right out of the text book.

NEW LOVE MAGAZINE, 1943

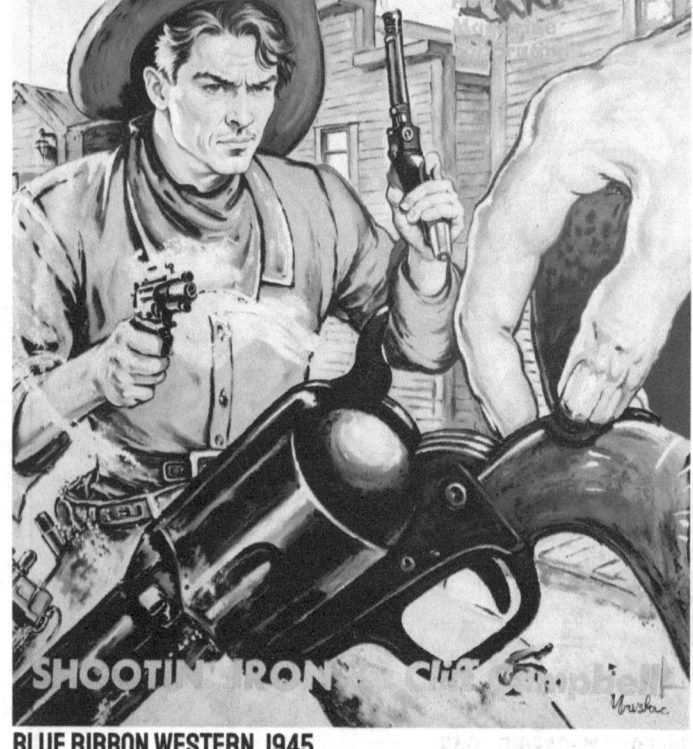

BLUE RIBBON WESTERN, 1945

5

FOR YOUR CHARACTERS AND the things that happen to them, of course, you've got to have a stage, a background. You will want the editor and the reader to see and believe this background so that the whole scene will seem real to him. This is one of the easiest tricks for you to learn. Yet, strangely enough, it is one of the weak spots of most beginning writers. They seem to be afraid of the words color and detail. Don't be. They are two of your best tools in the art of painting word pictures, which is exactly what you are doing when you write a story.

The method I always use, to achieve this realism

of background, I now pass on to you for what it is worth. You, with your words in a story, must become a motion picture camera that follows the action. As such, your words must not concentrate on the character, alone. You cannot treat the two separately, by slapping in a hunk of description in one spot and then forgetting about it. Blend your characters into that background description. This is what a motion picture camera does, as it follows a character about.

At the same time that you are going to play cameraman, you are also going to be your own director for this story scene. You can have trick lighting effects or all the dramatic props you want. You are going to be the sound effects man, too. You must, in giving a scene colorful, background detail, employ as many of the five senses as possible. Make your reader see, hear, feel, smell and if possible, taste everything.

That's not so hard. To use a quick example: in a story scene, your character sucks on a lemon. Don't say:

> He put the lemon into his mouth and sucked on it. It was sour.

Do say something like this:

> He put the lemon into his mouth. Suddenly his face twisted into a horrible grimace of distaste. He yanked the lemon from his mouth and hurled it in disgust to the floor.

Dramatize the thing. You don't have to tell the reader the lemon was sour. He knows that. But he wants to see the effect of that sourness on the character.

Here's another sample of what I mean by injecting color and detail into your background, in order to make what happens against that background more dramatic and real and believable to the reader. This is from a novelette of mine, called "Downbeat Dirge", soon to appear in Shock magazine.

This part of the story is being told, first person, by a young girl. She has been fighting with her lover on the edge of a cliff. Here's a slight idea of what can be done with this camera technique, in painting a background for your action, with words:

> I grabbed at him, but when I started to

go over the cliff my hand slipped away and all that I held onto was a leather button from his sport jacket. I saw the moon and the stars go rolling lazily, like a slow motion picture, around my head. I saw a nighthawk wheeling high above me. I remembered that the cliff was several hundred feet high and there was nothing but huge, jagged rocks at the bottom. The sound of my own screaming almost split my eardrums....

Folks, please, when you get into your background descriptions, from here on, in a story, load in that all-important color and detail. Don't be afraid of it. It's better for you to go too heavy than to skimp on it. This is one of the biggest troubles with most beginners' attempts at pulp fiction.

The story from which I've just quoted, by the way, has a rather interesting case history. I think it might serve as a good example for several other points on pulp writing.

You have probably noticed a slight, shall we say, tendency on my part toward non-conformity in the advice I've given you throughout this work. By now, if they've read this far, all the conformists in the business are probably squalling and squawking their heads off. They are yowling: "That's wrong, that's wrong! You can't write a story that way. It's liable to be rejected as too off-trail. Stick to the rules. A story has to do so-and-so and such-and-such and if it doesn't, it violates all the principles of blah, blah, blah!"

I say hogwash! You can write a story any damned way you feel like, providing you don't violate the one rule: make it entertaining! ... I'm assuming, of course, that you know a piece of commercial magazine fiction should not violate certain taboos of decency.

In fact the more you conform to a lot of out-dated Marquis of Queensbury rules for fiction writing, the more your story is going to be like ten thousand others and lost in the shuffle. The less it conforms, the more likely it is to be different, not dull and ordinary, but entertaining.

To get back to "Downheat Dirge". When I got the idea for this yarn, it seemed to me that the best way to tell it would be to break it up into four separate parts. Each part would be a different viewpoint. In other words, the whole story would be told in first person, but from four separate viewpoints. And not one of those viewpoints was that of the hero! In other words, a first person story, in which the hero does not enter at all, except as he affects the lives of these four people.

This struck me as a bit rugged. I have heard guys yap and yap that it is not good policy to change viewpoints once or twice, if you can possibly avoid it, and as a general rule I agree. And here I was thinking about doing it four times, even making the handling in that manner practically the whole idea of the story. It seemed risky, even to me.

I called my agent, Scott Meredith, in New York, discussed the idea with him. He groaned a little and muttered some remark about why hadn't he gone into the plumbing business or some such, and thought it over. Gradually, the idea began to appeal to him, too. He said:

"Let me call Harry Widmer and see how he reacts. That sounds like something he might like for Shock, his new magazine."

Okay. He called. Then he phoned me back. He said: "Bob, Harry says that he doesn't care how many viewpoints the damned thing has, so long as it's interesting and different. He says go ahead and try it and he'd like to see it and that it will not be rejected just because it happens to break a few rules. He says if it is strong and entertaining and dramatic and has the shock angle that he wants for that book, those are the only things that count."

Well, Harry Widmer bought that story and said that he liked the hell out of it. I said a little prayer of thanks that there was an editor who apparently didn't mind throwing away the rule book, too, if it was necessary.

And Mr. Widmer did not react that way because I wrote the story or because I use an agent, or for any silly reason like that. If he had never even heard of me and if the yarn had come into his office on the slush pile, cold, he still would have bought it.

And that last paragraph brings us to another subject: are all submitted manuscripts read? Why, seemingly, are some good stories rejected and some bad ones bought?

OUT OF THIS WORLD ADVENTURES, 1950

6

LET'S TAKE A LOOK inside the editorial rooms of a better class pulp publishing house. Let's take you behind the curtain for awhile and see the inner workings of this business. What makes magazines tick?

Where there is any large group of pulps, usually, the magazines are divided among a number of individual editors, who are under the direct supervision of one managing editor. These editors will usually be responsible for anywhere from two to four books a month. They get them out. They start from scratch and make up a magazine from absolutely nothing.

They are usually a bunch of pleasant, hard working guys and gals. All of them have had some previous editorial or publishing experience. Many of them can and do write damned good stories themselves. So don't get the idea that when you are unknown, your manuscript goes to a pulp house and some incompetent jerk is going to make the decision on it. This, except perhaps in very rare instances, is not true.

These pulp magazine editors start with a pile of manuscripts and build out of them the magazine that you finally see on your newsstand. Before anything else is done toward putting a magazine together, stories have to be read and bought! That is the big deal in a pulp editorial office. The rest is important and lots of hard work, buying the art, doing the blurbs and cover titles, "making up" the book, making title page layouts, reading proof, etc. But finding good stories is the big, important job. Without them there would be no magazine. So rest assured, your baby usually gets good treatment.

You finish a story and put it into the mail. Several days later, it hits the mail department of the publishing house to which it was sent. With others, it is sorted out and taken to the editorial office to which it was addressed. There the editor of that particular magazine puts those scripts which came in that mail on the bottom of one of two piles.

If your name, or the return address on the outside of the envelope, is known—that is, if you are a selling writer or have previously attracted attention because some other submission was close—your script will go into a rather small pile, made up of recent submissions of other known writers and of known agents.

If your name is not known—which makes your stuff an unknown quantity—the script is put at the bottom of the other pile, which is often huge. This is called the "slush" pile. It consists, I'm sorry to say, of about 98 percent junk. This is the fault of the writers, please understand, not the editors. It is also an advantage to you, if you have anything on the ball, because your script will then stand out like a rose on a garbage dump and the editor will make happy little noises.

Time is of utmost importance in an editorial office, as all magazines are gotten out under deadline conditions and printers and engravers cannot be kept waiting. So, when an editor is looking for stories with which to make up a magazine, he gives first attention to the "professional" pile of scripts. He does this because the odds are a thousand to one, at least, that he will find many more useable scripts in this pile than he will find in the "slush" heap.

On a day when there are no proofs to go out, no book to "make up," or perhaps when there are a couple of free hours at the end of the afternoon after these chores have been done, the editor will get to his reading. Sometimes, when conditions are very busy at the office, the editor is forced to do this reading on the train or bus that he takes home. Or at home. Understand, he usually gets no overtime pay for this. It is part of his job. Hereafter, please don't labor under the delusion that an editor does nothing but read manuscripts. Or that he is sitting there, just waiting for your script to come in. Nothing could be farther from the truth.

Anyhow, he gets to the "professional" pile. The casualties here are often heavier than you would expect them to be. Nearly all of these stories are "useable." That is, they are professional pieces of work, with not too many outstanding flaws. But the editor doesn't want merely "useable" stories. He wants damned good ones. He wants to get hold of a yarn that hits him so hard while he is reading it that he can hardly sit still. When he finishes reading he wants to be able to say: "Jesus, here's a hell of a good Smithers story!" This does not happen very often. It takes a wow of a story to get an editor excited. He's seen them all.

Thus he weeds out the best of the pro pile of scripts. Sometimes there might be half a dozen of these "best." Sometimes there is only one. Sometimes there is none. That is when an editor starts to work up a small ulcer. These "best," if the editor has full say and there is no managing editor, he will then buy. They are marked down in an editorial record book, vouchers for checks made out, etc. The stories are tentatively scheduled for future issues of magazines and then placed in the magazine's particular file, along with others. This file holds "available" manuscripts, "inventory" for future issues.

Sometimes, these files are practically empty. Say that there has been a dearth of good scripts. This thing will run in spells. Don't ask me why. But often there will be a stretch of time when practically no really good stories will come into the office. That is when agents get urgent phone calls from editors, screaming for copy. Or the editors will go madly tearing through piles of scripts, both the pro pile and the slush and in desperation, pull out a couple of a certain length, or a certain type.

That is when, three months after, you are liable to read a story in that particular magazine, that to you and to me smells to high heaven. You throw the book away in disgust and demand: "How can an editor buy junk like that? He must be a moron. What's the sense in my writing good stories, when they buy and publish bushwha like that?"

You've got something there, but not much. Keep your shirt on. Perhaps to you and me, that story smelled pretty loudly, but the chances are, in the period of desperation when it was earmarked for purchase, during a dearth of good scripts, it was probably the best of a sorry bunch. In other words, the editor had no choice.

Or perhaps it was of a certain length. Word lengths of stories play an important part in the pulp magazine business. Many magazines, because of the wording of the title of the book, have to use a certain number of stories in each issue. Like, let's say, 10-Story Cowboy magazine. The editor has to put ten stories in that magazine. He's got to run, usually, at least a couple of novelettes and four or five shorts of about 5,000 words each, plus a couple of short-shorts. This ropes him in pretty rigidly. It does not give him much room to move around with his story lengths. He probably has a top limit of from 10 to 12 thousand words for his novelettes. That means if he gets a story in his office, that is 18 or 20 thousand words, even though it might be a world-beater and he, personally, would think it the greatest piece of fiction in the world—he cannot run that story. He has to reject it.

The same thing applies to short stories. In order to squeeze a half dozen of them into an issue, he has to set a top word limit of, say, 5,000 words. So your story comes in, perhaps as good or slightly better than anything else in the pile, but it is 6,500 or 7,000 words long. With a sigh of regret, the editor rejects it. And you scream when it comes bouncing back to you.

Or let's say, he's got to have those short-shorts. He goes through every manuscript in the house, finds maybe ten scripts of the desired length. Of these ten, all of them are lousy. They reek. Believe me, this is quite possible. Thus, the editor has no alternative but to pick the best two or three of those stinkers and buy them.

That about answers the questions of why some bad stories are bought. The other answer, as to why good ones are sometimes rejected, follows right along.

At the opposite extreme to the dearth of good scripts, which we mentioned, there is sometimes a plethora of them. The editor upon occasion, has so many really wonderful stories in his manuscript piles, that he practically has to play eeny-meeny-mo to decide which ones to buy. Frequently, he buys them all. This flood of good material might last for several weeks and gurgling happily to himself, the editor goes on a big buying spree, as against the day when the flood will end and the famine begin once more. This will often result in a condition which is known in editorial offices as being "overstocked." At such a time, many really good stories go begging. They are rejected. And not because they aren't good enough.

Those are the fortunes of the writing racket. If you're a very lucky guy and happen to hit it just right, you'll sell a stinko story that you couldn't otherwise unload in a million years. If you're unlucky and hit it wrong, your perfectly good yarn will get the turndown.

There are several other minor reasons for these phenomena, but those are the big ones. It seems that everything goes in cycles with writers, usually. Either they are all turning out good scripts at the same time, or vice versa.

As for that "slush" pile. It is read from top to bottom. Or I should say, looked at. Your story might not be read all the way through. It isn't necessary for an editor to thus waste his time, usually. If your script is going to be very bad, a definite reject, he will spot this after reading the first few pages, or sometimes the first few paragraphs. If the scent is really terrific, after reading the first few lines.

On the other hand, if you've got stuff on the ball, it will show up almost immediately and the editor will continue to read as long as the story holds up. If it is pretty close, chances are he will encourage you by putting in a little note, instead of the usual printed rejection slip. But not always. Sometimes he doesn't have the time to do even this, no matter how much he wants to.

If your story is really good, if it measures right up to the standards of the scripts in the professional pile, and perhaps goes most of them one better, he'll buy. He'll be delighted to do so.

That's the way it goes, behind the scenes.

BLACK BOOK DETECTIVE, 1947

7

WE'LL DEAL BRIEFLY IN this chapter with the subject of dialogue. There has already been much said and much written on this subject. Surprisingly enough a great deal of it is good and true, and I will not bore you too much about it.

Dialogue is just a fancy name for talk. People talk. You know? Well, that's the way it is in a story. Don't get yourself all excited about this dialogue business. If you make your story characters talk the same way, approximately, that their counterparts in real life would do, you're on the right track. That is, the way those real life people would talk in a like situation. The only trouble with this is that most real life people don't get into too many story situations, so it will be hard for you to judge how they would talk. But you have imagination. If you haven't, you have a nerve, trying to learn how to write. Just use that imagination.

I've heard new writers counselled over and over with this sage advice: "Make your dialogue advance your story." That is another nice, pat bit of instruction that is sometimes taken too literally. I am a bit leery of putting it to you so baldly. After a writer has had this tidbit of textbook advice hurled at him, I've seen scripts written wherein every time a character opened his mouth, brother, does he advance that plot. But does he entertain? We're still holding doggedly to the fact that that is the full and final objective of every story and so, therefore, the same rule must apply to the various parts of said story.

The same things apply to dialogue as to other elements of your story. It must evoke an emotional response from your reader. There is, of course, no room for idle chit-chat in story dialogue and I suppose that is what is meant by, "Make dialogue advance your story." But perhaps it would be simpler if we put it this way: See to it that your characters' dialogue sticks pretty much to situations related to the story. There does, though, almost have to be certain little bits of irrelevant conversation in every story. You're trying to give an impression of realism. You can't have your characters talking like this:

He walked into the reception room and went up to the blonde girl at the desk. He said: "My name's Al Tracy. I'm here. to see Mr. Gibbons. I'm going to talk to him about an idea I've got that will save his company half a million dollars a year."

The girl looked up at him. She said: "You can't see him right now. He's busy. He's in conference. You should have called and made an appointment."

That dialogue advances the plot. It tells you about what Al Tracy is going to talk to Gibbons. That's about all it does. It is stilted and untrue to life. It gives you no particular picture of Tracy, the girl, or Gibbons. It is dull. It does not entertain. Try it this way:

He breezed into the knotty-pine-paneled reception room and swaggered over to the receptionist's desk. The girl behind the desk was small and blonde and cute, with her button nose and very red lips. Tracy said: "Hi, honey. Tell the big shot, inside, that Al Tracy's here to see him."

The blonde let her long-lashed blue eyes give Tracy

the once over. She suppressed a tiny smile of amusement. "I'm sorry, Mr. Tracy," she said. "But you can't see Mr. Gibbons right now. He's in conference. Did you have an appointment?"

Tracy poked out his full lower lip, frowned for a moment. Then he hiked a lean hip up onto the receptionist's desk. The frown disappeared. The slow lazy, boyish grin crept back over his face. He leaned forward confidentially. "Look, baby," he said. "You be a sweet kid and bust in there and tell the big boy that Al Tracy's got a little idea that will save his outfit a cool half million a year. I'll only take a minute of his time. You tell him it can't wait. You tell him—"

The baby blue eyes widened. "Oh, I couldn't do that," she cut Tracy off. "Mr. Gibbons flies into a terrible rage when he's interrupted. If I broke in on him now, he—he—well, there's no telling what he'd do."

Okay, that, roughly, is the difference. The second sample of dialogue also "advances the story." But it does—or should do—a hell of a lot more than that. Dialogue should help to characterize. It should tell you a few things about the characters who are talking. It should set the tone for the scene.

Again, we bring in the subject of emotions. They

affect the way people speak. Keep that in mind when you start off on a string of dialogue in your story. Talk is a giveaway on how people are feeling in real life. It should be the same way in stories.

For-instance, let's take some lines and tie them up with various emotions that the character who speaks is feeling at the time. See how it affects what he says and how he says it, although the subject matter remains the same. A guy goes into a bar and asks for a drink. This is one way the dialogue could go:

"I'll take a little rye. Straight, with water on the side, please."

"Sure thing. Any special kind of rye?

"Yeah. Morgan's if you've got it.".…

That's straight stuff. There are no particular emotions involved. The guy just wants a drink and the bartender is doing his job. Now let's try it like this:

"Give me a shot of rye and I want it straight, with a water chaser. Hurry it up. I ain't got all day."

"Take it easy. What kind of rye? I'm not a mind reader, you know."

"Morgan's! Morgan's, of course! What the hell kind of rye do you think?"…

That's rather obvious, isn't it? The customer is angry about something and he shows it in his dialogue.

The anger—the particular emotion shown in his dialogue lines—is contagious and the bartender answers in kind.

The way a person speaks usually reflects the type of person he is and the mood he is in at that particular time, or the emotion he is feeling. Keep that in mind when you write dialogue for your characters and you can't go far wrong. Make your dialogue stick pretty close to the story. Make it relevant, but make it human, the way an actual person will speak.

There isn't much more to say about dialogue that hasn't already been said, many times over. Since your dialogue issues from your story characters, the effect of the dialogue will depend on how well you have characterized your story people. If you have them well in hand and established as real-life, flesh and blood people, they will speak as such. They can hardly miss it. If they are merely wooden puppets, they will speak in stiff, awkward lines.

I would worry less about this subject of dialogue, if I were you, than I would about any of the other aspects of story writing. Master the rest of it and your dialogue will follow along like a nicely trained dog and never give you any trouble.

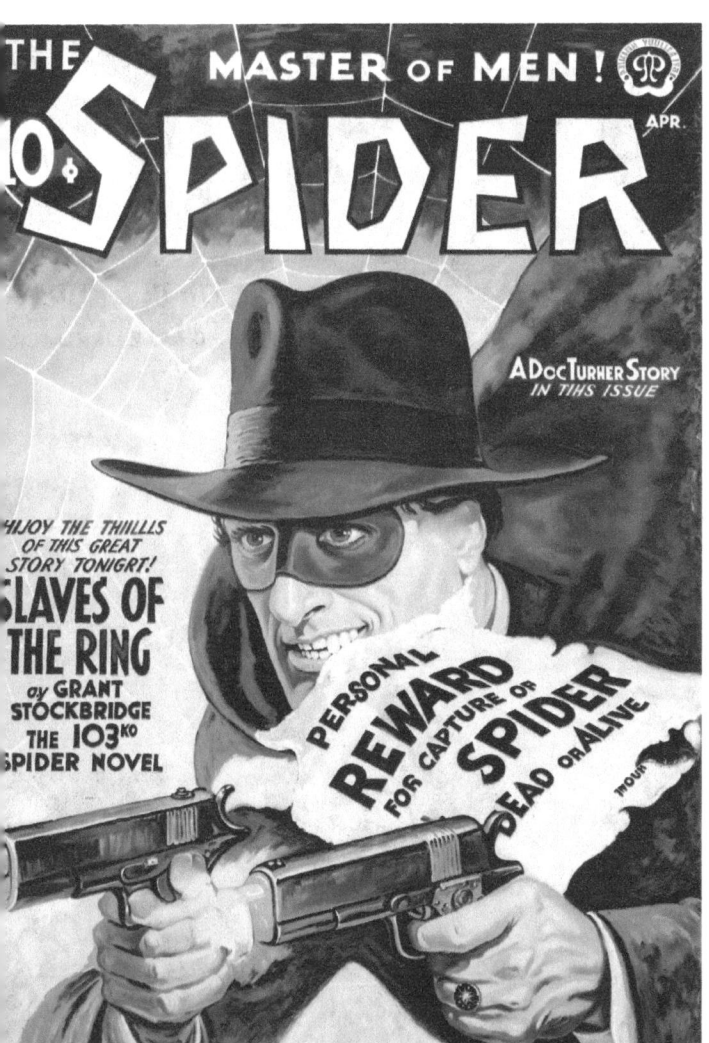

THE
MASTER OF MEN!
10¢ SPIDER APR.

A Doc Turner Story
IN THS ISSUE

ENJOY THE THIILLS
OF THIS GREAT
STORY TONIGRT!
SLAVES OF
THE RING
by GRANT
STOCKBRIDGE
THE 103ᴿᴰ
SPIDER NOVEL

PERSONAL REWARD FOR CAPTURE OF SPIDER DEAD OR ALIVE

SPIDER, 1942

THRILLING DETECTIVE

10¢

DEC.

DEATH IN A MURRY
A Exciting Novelry
By J. LANE LINKLATER

THE
MYSTERY MAN
OF SOHO
A Complere Crime Navel
By MARGERY ALLINGHAM

THRILLING DETECTIVE, 1946

8

SOMETHING THAT MAY GIVE you a little trouble is the subject of story lengths. You know that pulp magazines pay by the word and perhaps you figure: Why should I write short stories for fifty or seventy-five or a hundred dollars, when I can just as readily turn out novelettes for nice, juicy two hundred or three hundred dollar checks? That's a good question.

There are two answers, depending on your status as a pulp fiction writer, at the present time. If you're a newcomer, still trying to break in with your first story, I urgently recommend that you stick to the shorter lengths until you have at least a couple of sales under your belt. After you have made these sales, there's no reason at all why you shouldn't try the longer type of yarns.

There is good reason why the beginning writer stands a better chance of breaking in with short stories. There never seem to be enough really good shorts, under five thousand words, available in any of the pulp fields. This is because most of the "name" writers, the more experienced boys, want those larger checks. And also because, as experienced, battle-scarred vets in the fiction racket, they have usually been writing a long time. They do not any longer find ideas hanging from every bush. When they get hold of one, they do not like to use it up in a short story. So they embellish the thing, paint their picture on a larger canvas, worry that idea around until they can give it greater scope and work it into a novelette or short novel, instead of a short story. This way, they kill two birds with one stone. They get the larger check and they make one idea take the place of the two or three needed for short stories, to bring in the same amount of money.

Therefore, in the pulp short story field, your competition is a lot less keen. Some fine, experienced pulp writers continue to do shorts, long after they get a name and have learned how to turn out a really good story, but I would say they are in the minority. So there is one good, solid reason for sticking to shorts, in the beginning. Your chances for a sale are better.

Another reason is that shorts will be easier for you to do. If you make some mistakes, if you louse up an idea, there will not be so much time and effort wasted.

The shorter you make those early efforts, the better your chances will be. By the same token that the more experienced writers don't bother too much with shorts—and there is always a shortage of good ones in a pulp editorial office—so it applies that there is even a greater shortage of short-shorts. Very rarely does your full time pulp professional bother with these. The checks are too small. And again, the gag, upon which most short-shorts hinge, can be woven into a longer story, for a bigger check.

So as you go down the line on word lengths, the beginner's chances get better. There are many more 5,000 word short stories bought from the slush piles than there are 10,000 word novelettes. There are again as many more 2,500 and 3,000 word yarns bought as the 5,000 worders. And the short-shorts of 1,000 to 2,500 words are by far in the majority as break-in sales for new pulpsters.

In a short-short pulp story, the idea is of paramount importance. Usually, it hinges upon a twist ending, a gag. The characterization, atmosphere, mood, etc., are secondary considerations. Of course, if you add all those things to your main idea, the chances of selling even a short-short multiply a thousandfold. But the chances of making a lot of mistakes in a pulp short-short are not so great.

In a full length short story, you begin to need all the other elements of good writing. You can't get away with sketchy characterization and background as you can in the short-short.

So the program for the beginner, trying to break into the pulps is this: Concentrate on the shorts, first, from 1,000 words to, at the very top, 5,000 words. Then, like a bird, learning to fly, as you make a few sales of the very short ones, begin to spread your wings a little, take off on longer flights. Try the short novelettes next, the seven and eight thousand word yarns. And if you meet with success there, then you can step all the way up the ladder and take a crack at the ten, twelve, fifteen thousand word cover-feature novelettes and short novels.

There, again, is another good reason for the neophyte pulpster not to try the really long ones before he has sold something shorter. Rather, it increases the odds against his chances of selling. Because the real long stories usually are cover-featured and the pulps like to use established names on their covers. Names that the readers have become familiar with, whose stuff they like. Editors dislike taking a chance on a brand new name on their covers. Although they will do it upon rare occasion.

When you finally reach the point where you are ready to try the long stuff, if you have worked up to it, gradually, it probably won't give you too much trouble. You will find that there really isn't very much difference in the plotting and handling of the longer story.

As I mentioned before, in long novelettes, everything is painted on a broad canvas. You have to give your story scope. This means, for one thing, that in your climax, if, let's say, you are doing a western, instead of topping the yarn off with a shooting scene between the hero and the villain, as you would do in a short—in the longer story, you have the final gunsmoke showdown between two groups; you have a mass gunfight.

Everything is worked out on a larger scale in the

long novelette. You have more room to move around in and so, naturally, you will have many more scenes. You have more chance to build everything up, to give it more importance. This, naturally, takes a greater degree of craftsmanship. Instead of drawing a little word sketch, in the novelette you are painting a huge mural. You're going to have to paint with more and stronger colors, use more detail, all the way through.

All through this book, I haven't paid too much attention to the love pulp division. Perhaps it would be a good idea if I use that type of story now, to demonstrate more clearly what I mean in the difference between plotting a short and a novelette. Because it is easier, I will use for examples, some of my own published work in Rangeland Romances. Rangeland uses love stories against a background of the old west, but they are still essentially love stories.

In Rangeland stories, as in all of the love pulp field, the story is nearly always told from the girl's viewpoint. This is practically a rule. And much as I disapprove of rules, there isn't much I can do about this one. At least it didn't come from a textbook on writing. It is an editorial rule and that kind you do not buck.

In a love story, of course, the love problem of the

girl is the big thing. Always. In a Rangeland short of mine, here, roughly, is the plot: A pretty, love-starved young gal works in a cowtown cafe. She meets up with a handsome young cowpoke and falls for him. Every other guy in the town is nuts about her, but none of them appeal to her. This guy does, but he doesn't even seem to know she's alive. Actually, he is just bashful. There is a parrot in the story who plays a very important part. As a matter of fact, the parrot brings about the initial meeting of the guy and the gal. The guy owns the parrot and has brought him to town to get rid of him, on the orders of the ramrod at the ranch where he works. The boss of the cafe where the girl works is a fatherly old character, who feels sorry for this young couple who can't seem to get together. He realizes, wisely, that the guy's trouble is bashfulness and, with the aid of the parrot, he decides to play cupid. It is planted early in the story that this old guy is a mail order house gadget fan. Okay, he finally uses ventriloquism, learned from a mail order house book, to put words into the mouth of the parrot, which force the young cowpoke to show his true feelings.

That is, although very baldly stated, the plot of a love pulp story. It could have been a straight love yarn just as easily as it became a western romance. The scene could have been shifted to the East and the young cowpoke could have been made a brokerage office clerk or something. He could have been forced to get rid of the parrot by his rooming house landlady, instead of the foreman of the ranch and so forth. As I say, the same elements are used in all kinds of stories. And if you can plot, write and sell one type of pulp yarn, you can usually handle them all, or at least, a couple of the others.

But to get back to the difference between plotting a short and a novelette, you will notice that the plot I outlined for that short story, was very slight. It was small scale. It didn't have scope.

Now, we'll take a long novelette. You take the main background out of a small, peaceful cowtown, out of a small cafe. You ring in a lot more characters. You give the girl other problems beside the love one, but they must tie in with that love problem in some way, affect it.

In the long Rangeland novelette, the background was out on the open plains. The girl was a wagon train boss. In addition to her love problem with the hero, she had others. She had to get the huge wagon train safely through to its destination. She had to maintain discipline. To add to the love problem complications, we had to ring in not only another girl, but another man. To give the thing sweep and scope and importance, we brought in an Indian attack. But all these other elements are closely tied in with the main conflict and problem, as between the hero and the heroine. The hero in this instance, was a Texas cattleman who joins up with the wagon train as a shotgun guard.

Read and study your pulp novelettes and shorts and the differences in their plotting will become obvious. A good tipoff are your story illustrations in the pulps. For the short-shorts, you usually get a very small, spot illustration. For the full length shorts, you get a single page spread, usually containing only a simple scene. In your novelettes and short novels, you get a double-page-spread, featuring a big and important action scene of some kind. Well, those illustrations follow the story. In the shorts, you won't have any really big, terrific scenes. In your novelettes, you must have at least one.

It is perhaps something like a comparison between a movie short-subject film and the huge epic, super colossal feature length Hollywood spectacle.

PLANET STORIES, 1946

9

I HAVE BEEN SAVING some things for this last chapter which I think are a little bit special. I may be wrong. They may turn out to be duds and not work for you. But with other writers I have seen them accomplish almost miraculous results and I am rather surprised that these two, shall we say, *professional secrets*, are not more widely known, and used.

Before we get to them, though, I want first to touch lightly on the subject of production and of "forcing" stories. This is a big, debatable subject and one which professional pulpsters love to bat back and forth. Nobody seems to get anywhere with it, though. So that what I say here on the subject, is only my own opinion and it is quite possible that I am wrong as hell.

After you have sold a couple of dozen stories, you will come up against the problem and you will have to settle it in your own way. I'm just going to pass along a few personal ideas on the deal.

The only way that I know to achieve really high production—that is—to get up into the million word a year class in the pulps—is continually to force out stories and plots. This is done by a lot of writers. If you do it, you will make considerable money in the pulp field, that is, assuming that you have really learned how to write pulp stories. There are times, of course, when you have to do it, more or less. But I'm talking about making a steady thing of grinding and forcing out big pulp wordage, week after week, month after month, year after year.

If you're fairly young and a rugged soul, and have no aspirations toward the greener pastures of slick magazine sales, really heavy pulp production is all right for you. But I know of some heavy pulp producers who yearn like hell to make the slicks steadily. They would very much like to cut down on their wordage and, at the same time, increase their income. But they have become slaves to high production and never give themselves a chance to do this.

That can very easily happen. Once you've found an almost sure way to make yourself a thousand bucks a month, as some of these high production boys do, it is pretty difficult to slacken off, to take a chance on quality instead of quantity. Usually, as a writer's income goes up, so does his spending and he is, to a certain extent, trapped. It is a shame, too, because some of these high production pulpsters are really capable of turning out quality stuff. They could make the slicks steadily. They could get themselves the time to take a whack at the big sugar that comes from a hit novel. But heavy pulp production has got them in chains. As I said, some of them, of course, are happy in those chains and some of them aren't.

The point is that stories "forced" for heavy production, usually, are a rather mediocre product. They are not so apt to go over with the top-paying, better grade pulps. They are usually formula stuff. A writer continually doing this kind of a story does not give himself a chance really to work his story-writing skill up to the point where he's going to pound out a piece of work that is good enough for both pulp and slick. His products are usually rushed and therefore cannot help but show some signs of it. He cannot take time, nor the risk, to try going off-trail very much, or really smoothing and polishing up his characters and story situations to the point where they are good enough for both pulp and slick magazines.

So I advise the newcomer who wants to get some-place in this writing racket to go in for quality and not quantity in his pulp writing. You will remember that way back in the beginning, I said that you can write as fine stories as you want for the pulps. Provided they have a plot and fall within one of the pulp groups, no matter how good they are, the pulp editors will be glad to get them. You can't write too well for the pulps. You can write so well that the smooth paper magazines will like your stuff, too, and pay you much more for it.

You cannot do this, usually (I have to qualify these statements, otherwise somebody will come up and hit me in the face with an exception) if you concentrate on high production. I arrived at this conclusion by noticing that most of the pulp writers who have gone on and up and up, in the writing profession, put their efforts to quality and not quantity.

All this has not been as irrelevant to the opening paragraph as you might think. I mentioned there two little known facts about professional fiction writing;

perhaps they are even secrets. They seem so simple, now, that I almost hesitate to mention them. Yet, as an agent, when I told them to writers, time and again, they were amazed. And so was I, at the results.

The first thing is this: Relax, when you're writing your next story. By this, I don't mean to relax emotionally. You must stay pretty well keyed up, to write a really good yarn. But relax as far as trying to please some particular editor is concerned, in trying to write it the way you think he wants it written. I do not say this with any feeling of spite toward editors. I like editors. I've found them to be decent guys, as a group. And I do not think that editors are aware of this tendency on the part of writers to sweat and strain to please them, to give them what the writer thinks the editor wants—which is usually a story with all the ingredients he has found to be in the majority of the yarns that the editor uses in his particular magazine.

Relax and write a story, let's say, for your own amusement. If you are a writer with at least several sales under your belt, you are automatically and instinctively going to conform to some slight extent and that will get you by. You don't even have to think about it. Just write the best damned story that you can, putting into it all the new and different qualities of which you can think. Write a story the way you think it should be written, the kind of a story you would like to read. If you do your job well, you'll find it's a story you'll sell.

The second point is, "underplay" your writing. Use understatement. This is a favorite trick of good actors. Since your story characters are also actors, make them use this trick. You, as the author, should do it, also, in your description. If a guy, for instance, gets hurt in your story, if he gets shot, or stabbed or even punched in the nose—don't have gore splashing all over the place. Another word is "indirection."

For instance, say the hero throws a punch at the villain. There is a tendency to go at the scene the heavy, obvious and easiest way, to say:

> Jenson swung a punch up from the floor. It smashed full-force against Kelly's sneering mouth, knocked out several of his teeth and ribbons of crimson flowed from the corners of his mouth.

Instead, try something like this:

Jenson hit him. Kelly stumbled back-
ward. He shook his head and then he
put the palm of his hand to his mouth,
and took it away and stared stupidly at
the blood on it. The walls were blurry all
around him.

It's the same thing, but it is underplayed. You get the same feeling of the solid punch. You don't have to slam the reader over the head with a mallet to drive home a fact. Be subtle. If you want to show that a character is angry, don't necessarily have him jump up and down in a rage and pound his forehead with the heel of his hand. It's much more effective to call attention to the fact that his face suddenly went white with anger. Or have him suddenly crumple the letter he is reading and deliberately and carefully drop it into the waste basket. He doesn't have to shout with rage at the victim of his anger. If his voice drops to a strained whisper you can give the same impression.

The same thing applies to the emotion of sorrow. In fiction, as in real life, weeping and wailing and pulling out of the hair in handfuls does not always indicate the deepest grief. Sometimes the person who stands quietly, dry-eyed and abstractedly ripping a matchbook to pieces, is feeling the sorrow just as deeply.

Using both of these professional tricks can pay off big dividends. I have seen it happen again and again. The only thing I can't understand, is that some of the writers whom I have advised to try this, were amazed that they are "allowed" to do this, or that they had never thought of it, themselves.

One such instance, was the case of a writer by the name Alan Ritner Anderson and I hope he won't mind my using his name and one of his stories as an illustration. I hope he won't think I'm trying to steal his thunder and take credit for what happened. I'm not. Alan was a very, very fine writer before I ever knew him. He would have probably stumbled over these two "secrets" at some time or another, anyhow.

Alan Anderson came to me as a client when I was in the literary agency business. He had sold a number of pulp stories before the war. But since coming out of the Army, he'd been running into a little trouble. He'd been over-writing. He was splashing around too much gore and action. He was writing what he thought was the kind of story the pulp editors wanted and not the best sort of thing of which he was capable.

Right after I called his attention to these facts, and suggested that he try "underplaying" his stuff, "indirection," etc., and to forget the things a pulp story was supposed to contain and just turn out what he thought was one hell of a good yarn—well, Alan did just that. He sent me a story one bright afternoon. He accompanied this with a rather confused and unhappy note, saying that he liked the story, but he didn't suppose it had much chance, too off-trail and who the hell ever heard of a pulp crime yarn which was a love story and ghost story and murder story, all mixed in together, against a sort of historical background?

I sat down and read that thing and I couldn't sit still while I was reading it. It was that good. It had everything. It was a perfect example of underplayed, indirect writing. It was as different and off-trail as any story could possibly be. Alan had carried out my suggestions with a vengeance.

As an agent and as a writer, I had never in my life submitted anything to the Saturday Evening Post. But I sent this story to them, along with a short note explaining that I had never sent them anything before, because I'd never had anything that I thought was up to their standards. I thought this was. They did, too. They bought it like a flash, for $750, although it was a couple of thousand words longer than most of their short stories and although they do not go in too heavily for murder fiction in their shorts.

That off-trail story later was aired over national hookups. Several different foreign rights were sold. It was selected to appear in a volume of The Best Post Stories of 1947 and recently for the Dutton anthology, The Best Detective Stories of 1947. I suspect that the end is not yet, for that particular story. I still cannot understand why it has not been bought for pictures. It is a natural.

When I left the literary agency business and went back to freelancing, Alan Anderson teamed up with the same agent I picked and since then, Scott Meredith has pulled a repeat performance with one of Anderson's super special stories that was good enough for both pulp or slick and he hit the Post and radio sales, etc., again. This was another story that was damned well written the way Anderson thought it should be written, relaxed, not trying to follow formula and the well-worn trail of a lot of crime pulp yarns. This, too, was written with masterly "indirection" and "underplaying" of emotional reactions.

I have seen dozens of lesser successes along the same line, when other writers have done the same thing. I pass the word along, hoping that these "tricks" might be news to you, too, and that they will do you some good.

There isn't much more that I can tell you, that you haven't read someplace else. I could probably go on and on about this writing business. I know that I haven't covered everything here, by a long shot. I didn't try. I have tried to touch only on points and subjects that I believe have been overlooked to some extent in other books on writing. Particularly those applicable to writing for the pulp magazines.

I wish that I knew all there was to know about writing, so that I could tell it to you. I don't. Nobody does. There is so much to know and you never stop learning. So much of it is difficult to learn, too, to really get a grip on it. There are so many angles to it that are completely tenuous. That is one of the fascinating things about the profession. You can never stop learning and you can never really reach the top; you can always go just a little higher.

Good luck and happy writing!

The CASSOCK and the SWORD
By TOM W. BLACKBURN

MAMMOTH ADVENTURE, 1946